This book belongs to:

....

....

My Book of
ABC and 123

Parragon

Bath · New York · Singapore · Hong Kong · Cologne · Delhi · Melbourne

This edition published by Parragon in 2009

Parragon
Queen Street House
4 Queen Street
Bath BA1 1HE, UK

Photographer: Christopher Hornsby
Glass slipper photo by Shafer/Smith Photography

The edition containing "Bambi, A Life in the Woods" by Felix Salten is published by Simon & Schuster.

Tarzan® owned by Edgar Rice Burroughs, Inc., and used by permission;
© 1999 Edgar Rice Burroughs, Inc., and Disney Enterprises, Inc.

Toy Story 2 © 1999 Disney Enterprises, Inc., and Pixar Animation Studios.

Every effort has been made to contact all of the companies whose products appear in this book. Grateful acknowledgement is made to the following companies for permission to use their products: Bidegain S.A.; Converse; Cupcake Cafe; Duncan Toy Co.; Kmart Corporation; M & D Balloons; Maisto; Payless Shoe Source; Rayovac Corporation; Schylling Associates, Inc.; Spinmaster Toys; Tommy Hilfiger; Trim Foot Co.; Williams-Sonoma/Pottery Barn; Umbra, Inc.

Matchbox® is a trademark of Mattel, Inc. Hot Wheels ® and associated trademarks are owned by and used by permission from Mattel, Inc. © 1998 Mattel, Inc. With the exception of the trademark used by permission, Mattel, Inc., is not affiliated with this book. Playing card faces depicted herein under authorization of the United States Playing Card Company, Cincinnati, Ohio 45212, USA.

ISBN 978-1-4075-5464-8
Printed in China

ABC

ABC

Note to Parents

Young children will have lots of fun learning the letters of the alphabet and the sounds they make.

This lively and entertaining introduction to the alphabet has been especially created to introduce letter names and sounds. Your child will love spotting pictures of favourite Disney characters while learning to recognise the words associated with them.

Enjoy sharing this magical experience as your child takes the first steps into the wonderful world of letters and words.

a b c d e f g h i j k l m n o p q r s t u v w x y z

A a

aeroplane

apple

a b c d e f g h i j k l m n o p q r s t u v w x y z

Bb

Bambi

Belle

ball

bananas

balloons

bowl

bow

a b c d e f g h i j k l m n o p q r s t u v w x y z

a b c d e f g h i j k l m n o p q r s t u v w x y z

Cc

Cinderella

Cruella

cat

candle

crown

car

clock

a b c d e f g h i j k l m n o p q r s t u v w x y z

a b c d e f g h i j k l m n o p q r s t u v w x y z

Dumbo

Dd

Daisy

dog

doughnut

dress

duck

drum

a b c d e f g h i j k l m n o p q r s t u v w x y z

Ee

Eeyore

Esmeralda

earrings

elephant

egg

eye

envelopes

a b c d e f g h i j k l m n o p q r s t u v w x y z

a b c d e f g h i j k l m n o p q r s t u v w x y z

Ff

Flik

Fairy Godmother

football

flower

fork

feather

flag

a b c d e f g h i j k l m n o p q r s t u v w x y z

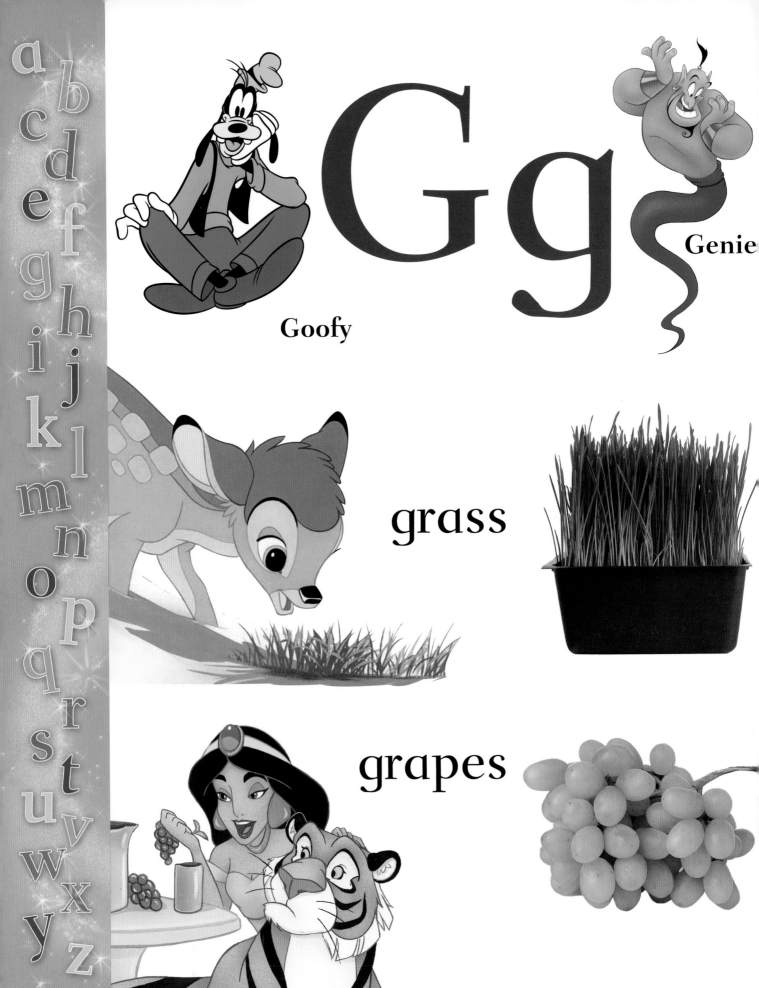

a b c d e f g h i j k l m n o p q r s t u v w x y z

Gg

Goofy

Genie

grass

grapes

gloves

goat

goldfish

a b c d e f g h i j k l m n o p q r s t u v w x y z

Hades

Hh

Hercules

hat

hammer

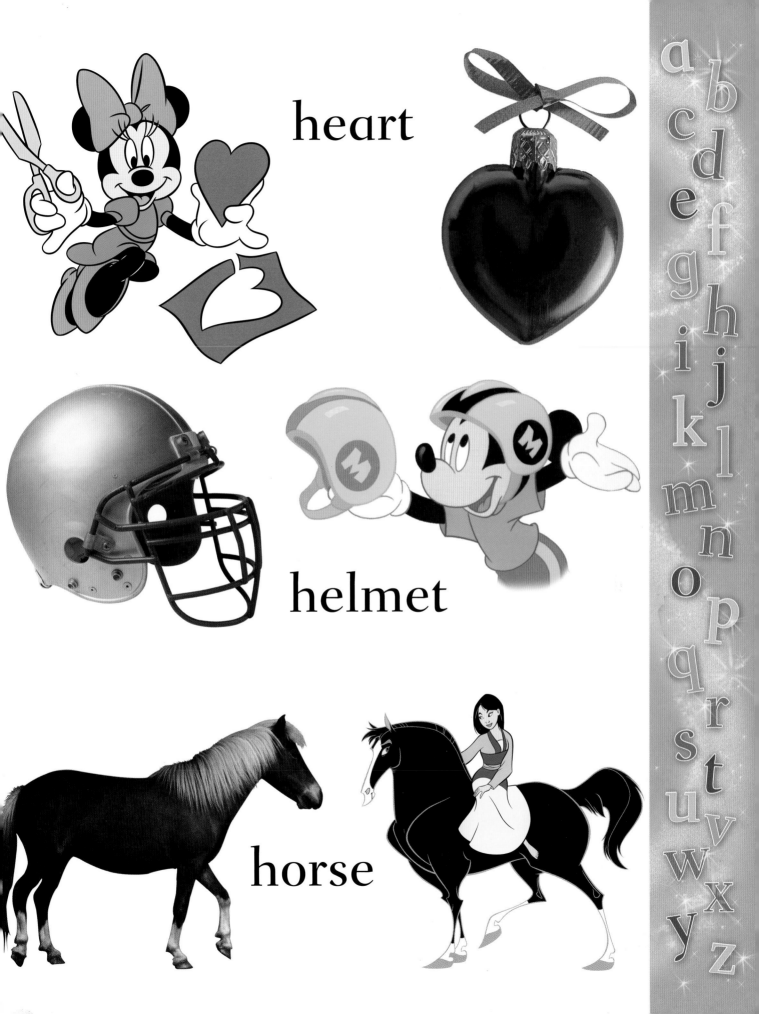

heart

helmet

horse

a b c d e f g h i j k l m n o p q r s t u v w x y z

Iago

Ii

ice-cream

J j

Jiminy Cricket

jar

jack-in-the-box

a b c d e f g h i j k l m n o p q r s t u v w x y z

a b c d e f g h i j k l m n o p q r s t u v w x y z

Kanga

Kaa

Kk

kite

keys

knife

kitten

king

a b c d e f g h i j k l m n o p q r s t u v w x y z

Lady

Ll

lion

ladybird

Mm

Mickey Mouse

monkey

mouse

a b c d e f g h i j k l m n o p q r s t u v w x y z

Nala

Nn

necklace

nest

Oo

Oliver

orange

owl

a b c d e f g h i j k l m n o p q r s t u v w x y z

Peter Pan

Pp

pillow

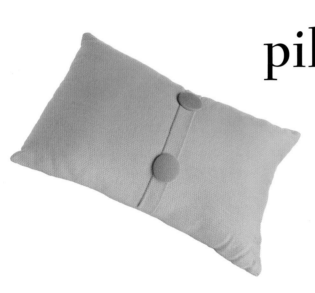

plate

a b c d e f g h i j k l m n o p q r s t u v w x y z

Qq

Quasimodo

queen

quill

a b c d e f g h i j k l m n o p q r s t u v w x y z

a b c d e f g h i j k l m n o p q r s t u v w x y z

Rr

Rafiki

Robin Hood

rose

ribbon

raincoat

rabbit

rope

a b c d e f g h i j k l m n o p q r s t u v w x y z

a b c d e f g h i j k l m n o p q r s t u v w x y z

Ss

Simba

Sultan

sunglasses

shell

shirt

spoon

shoes

a b c d e f g h i j k l m n o p q r s t u v w x y z

a b c d e f g h i j k l m n o p q r s t u v w x y z

 **T t**

Thumper

Tigger

torch

teacup

tiger

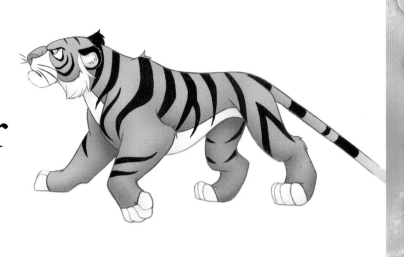

teeth

toothbrush

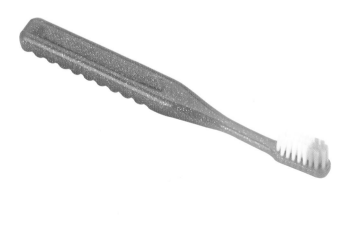

a b c d e f g h i j k l m n o p q r s t u v w x y z

Uu

Ursula

umbrella

underwear

Vv

Victor

vase

violin

a b c d e f g h i j k l m n o p q r s t u v w x y z

Ww

a b c d e f g h i j k l m n o p q r s t u v w x y z

Woody

White Rabbit

window

watch

watermelon

watering can

wings

a b c d e f g h i j k l m n o p q r s t u v w x y z

eXcalibur

xylophone

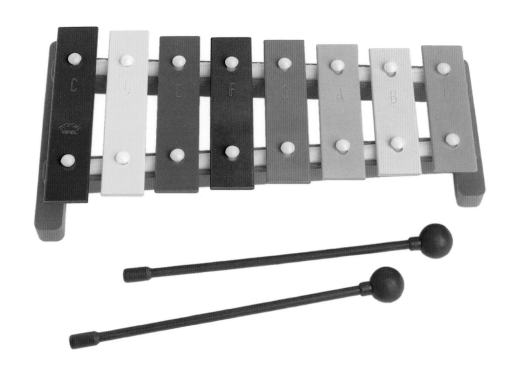

Yy

Yao

yo-yo

a
b
c
d
e
f
g
h
i
j
k
l
m
n
o
p
q
r
s
t
u
v
w
x
y
z

Zazu

Zz

zebra

a b c d e f g h i j k l m n o p q r s t u v w x y z

The alphabet

 a is for aeroplane

 n is for nest

b is for balloon

o is for owl

c is for cat

p is for pillow

d is for dog

q is for queen

e is for elephant

r is for rabbit

f is for football

s is for sunglasses

g is for goat

t is for tiger

h is for hat

u is for umbrella

i is for ice-cream

v is for violin

j is for jack-in-the-box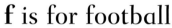

w is for window

k is for king

x is for xylophone

l is for lion

y is for yo-yo

m is for mouse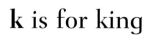

z is for zebra

Look at the first letter below.
Say the letter out loud. Can you find a picture
that begins with the same sound?
Now do the same for the other letters.

a b h k p o r t

Name the pictures in each row.
Two of the pictures begin with the same letter.
Point to the picture in each row that begins with a different letter.

The first letter of each word below is missing.
Look carefully at each picture and then say the missing
letter out loud.

_all

_uck

_ammer

_ite

_atch

1 2 3

123

Note to Parents

Numbers are fun – and that's the most important mathematical concept every young child needs to learn!

Developed in association with a child-development expert, this entertaining and vibrant introduction to numbers and counting has been created especially for you to share with your child.

The magic and laughter that young children associate with their favourite Disney characters can be part of their first steps into the world of early maths.

Cinderella lost a glass slipper when she left the ball. How many slippers can you see?

1
2
3
4
5
6
7
8
9
10
11
12
13
14
15
16
17
18
19
20

2

"Mickey and Minnie are my best friends!" says Goofy. How many of Goofy's friends can you count here?

Cinderella's mice friends made her a dress for the ball. How many reels of cotton did they use?

3

1 2 3 4 5 6 7 8 9 10 11 12 13 14 15 16 17 18 19 20

4

Lady loves good food, and Tramp does too! How many bowls of delicious spaghetti can you see?

Pinocchio takes a shiny red apple to school. He doesn't like green apples at all! How many green apples did he leave behind?

5

1
2
3
4
5
6
7
8
9
10
11
12
13
14
15
16
17
18
19
20

1
2
3
4
5
6
7
8
9
10
11
12
13
14
15
16
17
18
19
20

6

Donald's favourite lunch is pizza. How many slices of pizza will he eat today?

The dwarfs have left their lunch boxes in the cottage. How many boxes can you count? And how many dwarfs?

7

1 2 3 4 5 6 7 8 9 10 11 12 13 14 15 16 17 18 19 20

8 Ariel loves to collect shells in the sea. How many shells does she have?

Cinderella has lots of shoes
as well as one glass slipper.
How many shoes can you
count altogether?

9

1
2
3
4
5
6
7
8
9
10
11
12
13
14
15
16
17
18
19
20

1
2
3
4
5
6
7
8
9
10
11
12
13
14
15
16
17
18
19
20

10

Mickey Mouse hates peas. How many did he leave on his plate?

Hercules loves to eat fruit – it keeps him strong and healthy. How many pieces of fruit can you count?

11

1
2
3
4
5
6
7
8
9
10
11
12
13
14
15
16
17
18
19
20

12

Belle loves to read books! How many books can you see here?

Disney's Winnie the Pooh's **Play-Along Rhymes**

Disney's **Lessons from the Hundred-Acre Wood**

Disney's *Princess Collection* DISNEY PRESS

SABUDA **ABC DISNEY** DISNEY PRESS

The Many Adventures of Winnie the Pooh: A Classic Disney Treasury DISNEY PRESS

Storybook Collection

Celebrate the Year with Winnie the Pooh: A Disney Holiday Treasury DISNEY PRESS

Disney's **EASY-TO-READ STORIES** Disney

The New Illustrated TREASURY OF Disney SONGS

MY VERY FIRST *Disney* ABC WORD BOOK

Disney's **TARZAN** DISNEY PRESS

Disney's *Family Story Collection* DISNEY PRESS

Abu goes bananas for bananas! How many does he have here?

13

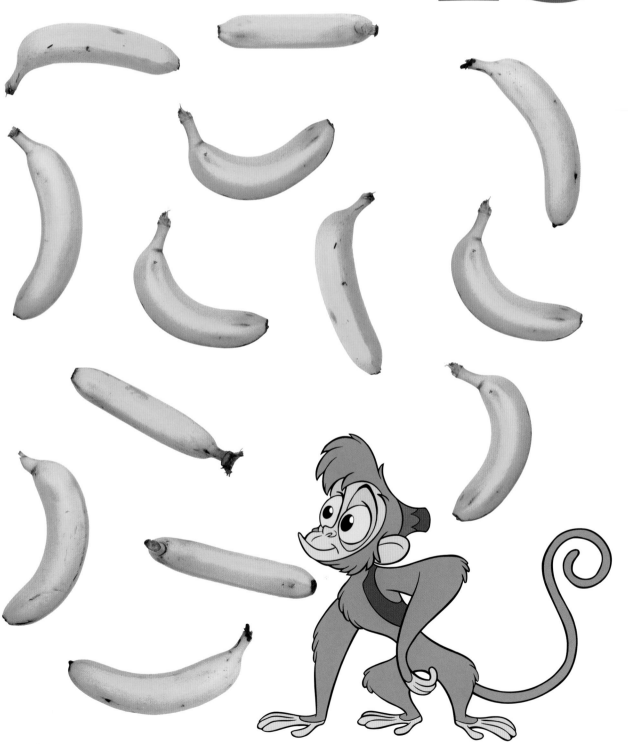

1 2 3 4 5 6 7 8 9 10 11 12 13 14 15 16 17 18 19 20

14

It's Daisy's birthday. How many presents has Donald wrapped for her?

Tarzan and Jane make friends with lots of animals. How many birds can you see?

15

1 2 3 4 5 6 7 8 9 10 11 12 13 14 15 16 17 18 19 20

16

Jiminy Cricket thinks hats are great! How many hats can you count? Don't forget the one in Jiminy's hand!

Alice loves to wear pretty ornaments in her hair. How many can you see?

17

1 2 3 4 5 6 7 8 9 10 11 12 13 14 15 16 17 18 19 20

18

Donald and Mickey like anything that goes fast. How many vehicles have they collected?

How many motorcycles can you spot?

Daisy and Donald spent all afternoon baking cookies. How many did they make?

19

1
2
3
4
5
6
7
8
9
10
11
12
13
14
15
16
17
18
19
20

20

Mickey loves balloons. How many can you count.

How many Mickey Mouse balloons can you find?

Goofy loves to eat cupcakes. How many does he have here?

30

40

Mufasa was the first king of the Pride Lands. How many of his subjects can you count here? Don't count Mufasa, Simba and Nala!

How many birds can you spot?

1
2
3
4
5
6
7
8
9
10
11
12
13
14
15
16
17
18
19
20

1
2
3
4
5
6
7
8
9
10
11
12
13
14
15
16
17
18
19
20

50

Alice wants to play cards
with the Queen of Hearts
How many cards does
Alice have?

60

Mickey and Minnie have lots of sweets! How many can you count altogether?

1
2
3
4
5
6
7
8
9
10
11
12
13
14
15
16
17
18
19
20

70

The Little Green Army Men are coming to help Buzz and Woody. Can you count them all?

80

Mickey loves to draw pictures. How many crayons does he have?

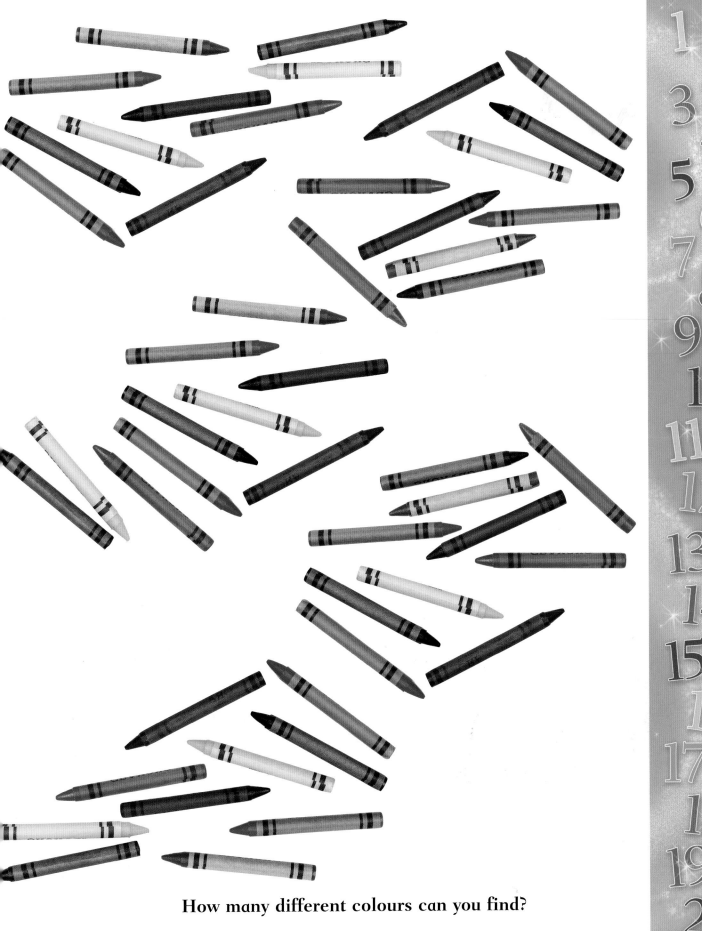

How many different colours can you find?

1
2
3
4
5
6
7
8
9
10
11
12
13
14
15
16
17
18
19
20

90

Flower loves to smell flowers. How many can you find? Don't count the ones Flower is sitting on!

1
2
3
4
5
6
7
8
9
10
11
12
13
14
15
16
17
18
19
20

100

Belle loves to hang ornaments on her Christmas tree. How many can you count?

1,000

Tinker Bell spreads her magic fairy dust wherever she goes. There are 1000 sparkles on these two pages! Can you count them all?

1
2
3
4
5
6
7
8
9
10
11
12
13
14
15
16
17
18
19
20

Numbers 1 to 20

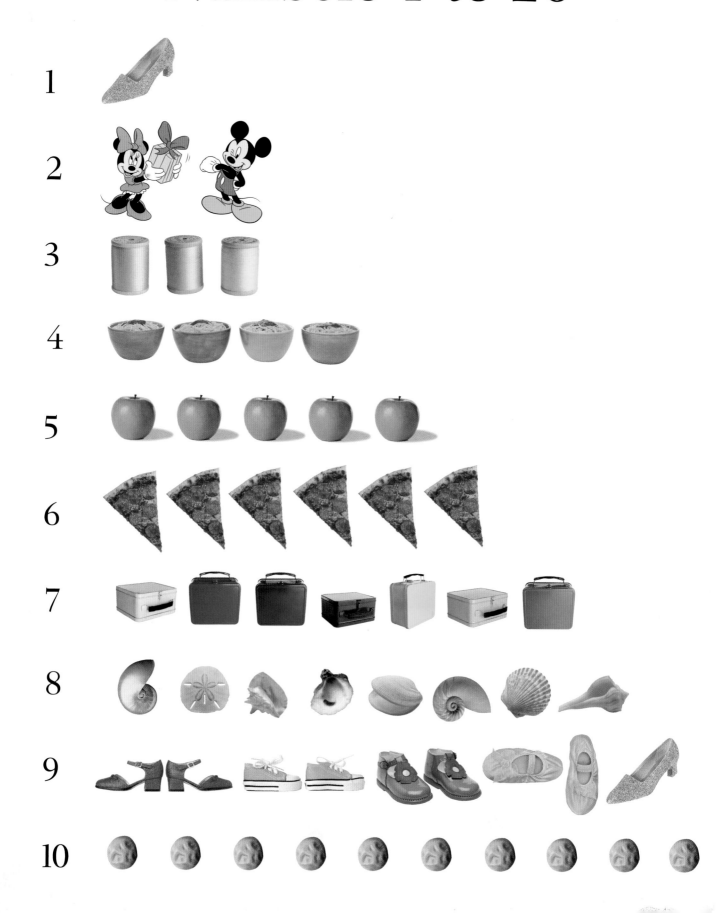

1

2

3

4

5

6

7

8

9

10

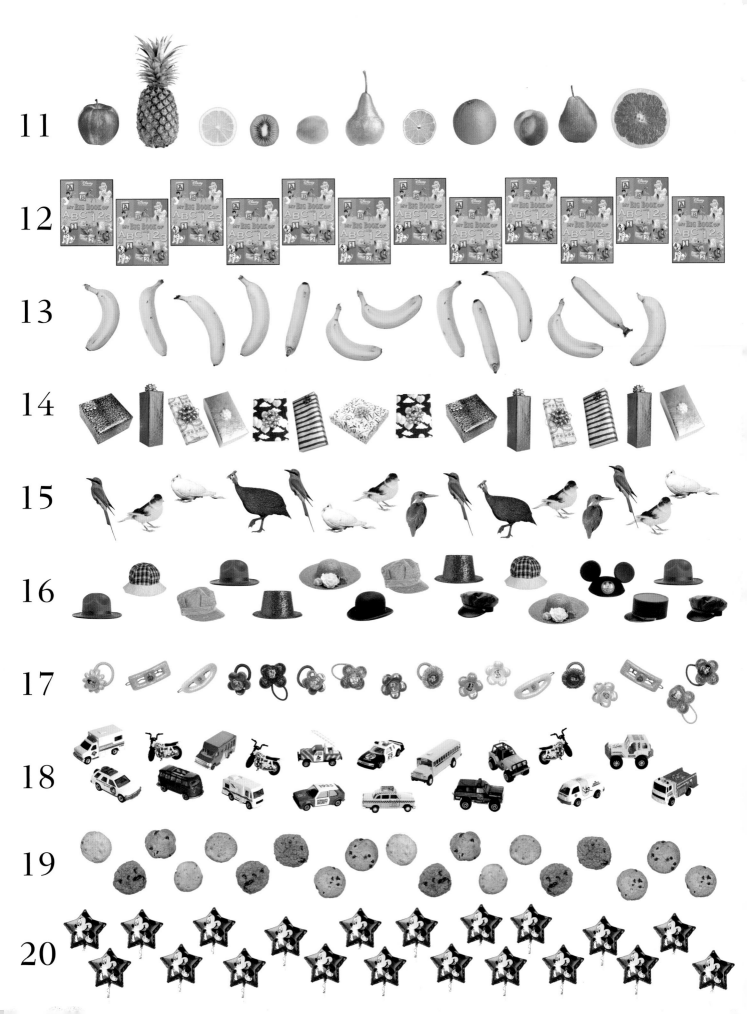

Count the number of things in each group.
Look at the numbers below and point to the one that matche
your answer.

2 3 4

4 5 6

3 4 5

5 6 7

How many things can you count in each group?
Now point to the number that matches each answer.

3 7 4 2 6 5